D0734805

ALL WILL
BE WELL

To Colin & Allie Mar 17, 2021
for no special reason
love Dad

ALL WILL BE WELL

GOOD ADVICE FROM WINSTON CHURCHILL

This edition published 2011
First published in 2011 by Ebury Press, an imprint of Ebury Publishing
A Random House Group company

The Random House Group Limited Reg. No. 954009

Addresses for companies within the Random House Group can be found at www.randomhouse.co.uk

A CIP catalogue record for this book is available from the British Library

Penguin Random House is committed to a sustainable future for our business, our readers and our planet. This book is made from Forest Stewardship Council® certified paper.

Designed and set by seagulls.net

Printed in the UK by Clays Ltd, St Ives plc

ISBN 9780091941499

To buy books by your favourite authors and register for offers visit www.randomhouse.co.uk

CONTENTS

LIVE DANGEROUSLY; TAKE THINGS AS THEY COME; DREAD NAUGHT, ALL WILL BE WELL.

1932

INTRODUCTION

Sir Winston Churchill was prime minister of Great Britain in the years 1939–1945 and 1951–55. He was a great orator whose speeches reassured and inspired the country through some of the darkest days of the Second World War. One of history's most remarkable leaders, he could be witty, dry, rousing and wise. He had a deserved reputation for

lightning parries and razor-edged thrusts at critics, and could be a terrifying opponent at Prime Minister's Question Time, and yet his love of language made him a gifted communicator.

Why do we still find his words so relevant today? Churchill has much to tell us about the element of chance, the inevitability of mistakes, and the certainty of disappointments before victory is won. Charisma has something to do with it: and that he achieved victory despite the odds, with humour and gusto.

Many of his quips and witticisms have become legendary, yet nothing surpasses his famous speeches of 1940 that rallied a nation threatened with invasion when there was little with which to fight. Ronald Golding, one of Churchill's Scotland Yard bodyguards in 1946, was an RAF squadron leader when he first heard the famous voice, crackling over the

ether on the wireless. 'After those speeches,' he said, 'we wanted the Germans to come.'

Churchill urged Britain to fight with 'might and main', which often makes people regard him purely as a warrior. But no patriot held a more overriding desire for peace, and Churchill strove to avoid both great wars of the last century. Once war had begun however, his precepts were simple: take the initiative, accept risk, prefer action to inaction, and never surrender.

He accepted blame or criticism with equal grace, and was decisive, as any great leader should be, but never impervious to argument. He generally kept an open mind, and was ready to follow advice from people whose judgement he trusted. However, when he had made up his mind, it was difficult to persuade him to change it. Two of his favourite sayings were: 'I would sooner be right than consistent' and 'In the

course of my life I have often had to eat my words, and I must confess that I have always found it a wholesome diet.'

The quotations here are but a small selection. Over a long life, Churchill offered so much advice that compiling a list of his maxims is a formidable task. All items in *All Will Be Well* can be attributed to Winston Churchill, and they are all republished here with the permission of his Literary Estate.

HOW TO
SUCCEED

NO ONE SHOULD WASTE A DAY.

1948

A HOPEFUL DISPOSITION IS NOT THE SOLE QUALIFICATION TO BE A PROPHET.

1927

NEVER SUBMIT TO FAILURE.

1930

YOU MUST PUT YOUR HEAD INTO THE LION'S MOUTH IF THE PERFORMANCE IS TO BE A SUCCESS.

1900

EVERY MAN SHOULD ASK HIMSELF EACH DAY WHETHER HE IS NOT TOO READILY ACCEPTING NEGATIVE SOLUTIONS.

1918

IT IS NO USE SAYING, 'WE ARE DOING OUR BEST.' YOU HAVE GOT TO SUCCEED IN DOING WHAT IS NECESSARY.

1916

THERE IS NOTHING WRONG IN CHANGE, IF IT IS IN THE RIGHT DIRECTION. TO IMPROVE IS TO CHANGE, SO TO BE PERFECT IS TO HAVE CHANGED OFTEN.

1925

ALLOWANCE MUST BE MADE FOR THE INTERVENTION OF THE UNEXPECTED.

1923

CRITICISM IN THE BODY POLITIC IS LIKE PAIN IN THE HUMAN BODY. IT IS NOT PLEASANT, BUT WHERE WOULD THE BODY BE WITHOUT IT?

1940

THERE IS ALWAYS MUCH TO BE SAID FOR NOT ATTEMPTING MORE THAN YOU CAN DO, AND FOR MAKING A CERTAINTY OF WHAT YOU TRY. BUT THIS PRINCIPLE, LIKE OTHERS IN LIFE AND WAR, HAS ITS EXCEPTIONS.

1941

WE MUST NOT LOSE OUR FACULTY TO DARE, PARTICULARLY IN DARK DAYS.

1942

SOMETIMES WHEN [FORTUNE] SCOWLS MOST SPITEFULLY, SHE IS PREPARING HER MOST DAZZLING GIFTS.

1931

IF WE LOOK BACK ON OUR PAST LIFE WE SHALL SEE THAT ONE OF ITS MOST USUAL EXPERIENCES IS THAT WE HAVE BEEN HELPED BY OUR MISTAKES.

1931

PATIENCE, HOWEVER, AND GOOD TEMPER ACCOMPLISH MUCH.

1912

IT IS MUCH BETTER TO SET UP AN OBJECTIVE, EVEN IF IT BE BEYOND YOUR REACH, THAN IT IS TO GIVE UP THE STRUGGLE AT THE OUTSET.

1927

**NEVER GIVE IN,
NEVER, NEVER, NEVER,
NEVER – IN NOTHING,
GREAT OR SMALL,
LARGE OR PETTY –
NEVER GIVE IN EXCEPT
TO CONVICTIONS
OF HONOUR AND
GOOD SENSE.**

1941

SUCCESS ALWAYS DEMANDS A GREATER EFFORT.

1940

THE BUSINESS OF LIFE

IT IS VERY MUCH BETTER SOMETIMES TO HAVE A PANIC FEELING BEFOREHAND, AND THEN BE QUITE CALM WHEN THINGS HAPPEN, THAN TO BE EXTREMELY CALM BEFOREHAND AND TO GET INTO A PANIC WHEN THINGS HAPPEN.

1935

WE HAVE ALWAYS TO BE ON OUR GUARD AGAINST BEING THROWN OFF OUR TRUE COURSE BY CHANCE AND CIRCUMSTANCE.

1931

CHANGE IS THE MASTER KEY. A MAN CAN WEAR OUT A PARTICULAR PART OF HIS MIND BY CONTINUALLY USING IT AND TIRING IT, JUST IN THE SAME WAY AS HE CAN WEAR OUT THE ELBOWS OF HIS COAT.

1925

WHEN DANGER IS FAR OFF WE MAY THINK OF OUR WEAKNESS; WHEN IT IS NEAR WE MUST NOT FORGET OUR STRENGTH.

1939

SOME PEOPLE WILL DENY ANYTHING, BUT THERE ARE SOME DENIALS THAT DO NOT ALTER THE FACTS.

1910

ONLY ONE LINK IN THE CHAIN OF DESTINY CAN BE HANDLED AT A TIME.

1945

THE LONGER YOU CAN LOOK BACK, THE FARTHER YOU CAN LOOK FORWARD.

1944

OUT OF INTENSE COMPLEXITIES, INTENSE SIMPLICITIES EMERGE.

1927

THINGS DO NOT GET BETTER BY BEING LET ALONE. UNLESS THEY ARE ADJUSTED, THEY EXPLODE WITH A SHATTERING DETONATION.

1927

UNITED WISHES AND GOODWILL CANNOT OVERCOME BRUTE FACTS.

1951

EVEN [MAN'S] GREATEST NEGLECTS OR FAILURES MAY BRING HIM GOOD. EVEN HIS GREATEST ACHIEVEMENTS MAY WORK HIM ILL.

1936

IN MY EXPERIENCE OF LARGE ENTERPRISES, I HAVE FOUND IT IS OFTEN A MISTAKE TO TRY TO SETTLE EVERYTHING AT ONCE. FAR OFF, ON THE SKYLINE, WE CAN SEE THE PEAKS OF THE DELECTABLE MOUNTAINS. BUT WE

CANNOT TELL WHAT LIES BETWEEN US AND THEM. WE KNOW WHERE WE WANT TO GO; BUT WE CANNOT FORESEE ALL THE STAGES OF THE JOURNEY, NOR CAN WE PLAN OUR MARCHES AS IN A MILITARY OPERATION.

1947

WE MUST LEARN TO BE EQUALLY GOOD AT WHAT IS SHORT AND SHARP AND WHAT IS LONG AND TOUGH.

1941

THE MAXIM 'NOTHING AVAILS BUT PERFECTION' MAY BE SPELT SHORTER: 'PARALYSIS'.

1942

IT IS WONDERFUL HOW WELL MEN CAN KEEP SECRETS THEY HAVE NOT BEEN TOLD.

1900

THE BEST EVIDENCE OF THE FAIRNESS OF ANY SETTLEMENT IS THE FACT THAT IT FULLY SATISFIES NEITHER PARTY.

1926

THE PROBLEMS OF VICTORY ARE MORE AGREEABLE THAN THOSE OF DEFEAT, BUT THEY ARE NO LESS DIFFICULT.

1942

HOW
TO LIVE

LIFE, WHICH IS SO COMPLICATED AND DIFFICULT IN GREAT MATTERS, NEARLY ALWAYS PRESENTS ITSELF IN SIMPLE TERMS.

1941

ALL THE GREATEST THINGS ARE SIMPLE, AND MANY CAN BE EXPRESSED IN A SINGLE WORD: FREEDOM; JUSTICE; HONOUR; DUTY; MERCY; HOPE.

1947

IN LIFE'S STEEPLECHASE ONE MUST ALWAYS JUMP THE FENCES WHEN THEY COME.

1930

FEARTHOUGHT IS FUTILE WORRYING OVER WHAT CANNOT BE AVERTED OR WILL PROBABLY NEVER HAPPEN.

1937

THERE LIES BEFORE [MANKIND], AS HE WISHES, A GOLDEN AGE OF PEACE AND PROGRESS. ALL IS IN HIS HAND. HE HAS ONLY TO CONQUER HIS LAST AND WORST ENEMY – HIMSELF.

1950

WE MUST ALWAYS BE READY TO MAKE SACRIFICES FOR THE GREAT CAUSES; ONLY IN THAT WAY SHALL WE LIVE TO KEEP OUR SOULS ALIVE.

1948

COURAGE IS RIGHTLY ESTEEMED THE FIRST OF HUMAN QUALITIES BECAUSE, AS HAS BEEN SAID, IT IS THE QUALITY WHICH GUARANTEES ALL OTHERS.

1931

WE CANNOT UNDO THE PAST, BUT WE ARE BOUND TO PASS IT IN REVIEW IN ORDER TO DRAW FROM IT SUCH LESSONS AS MAY BE APPLICABLE TO THE FUTURE.

1936

NOTHING SHOULD BE DONE FOR SPITE'S SAKE.

1944

AS LONG AS THE JOB IS DONE, IT DOES NOT MATTER MUCH WHO GETS THE CREDIT.

1942

DEATH IS THE GREATEST GIFT THAT GOD HAS MADE TO US.

1943

YOU MUST SLEEP SOME TIME BETWEEN LUNCH AND DINNER, AND NO HALF-WAY MEASURES. TAKE OFF YOUR CLOTHES AND GET INTO BED. THAT'S WHAT I ALWAYS DO. DON'T THINK YOU WILL BE DOING LESS WORK BECAUSE YOU SLEEP

DURING THE DAY. THAT'S A FOOLISH NOTION HELD BY PEOPLE WHO HAVE NO IMAGINATION. YOU WILL BE ABLE TO ACCOMPLISH MORE. YOU GET TWO DAYS IN ONE – WELL, AT LEAST ONE AND A HALF, I'M SURE.

1946

HOW LITTLE WE SHOULD WORRY ABOUT ANYTHING EXCEPT DOING OUR BEST.

1951

LET US RECONCILE OURSELVES TO THE MYSTERIOUS RHYTHM OF OUR DESTINIES, SUCH AS THEY MUST BE IN THIS WORLD OF SPACE AND TIME.

1931

THE FUTURE IS UNKNOWABLE, BUT THE PAST SHOULD GIVE US HOPE.

1958

HOW LITTLE CAN WE FORESEE THE CONSEQUENCES EITHER OF WISE OR UNWISE ACTION, OF VIRTUE OR OF MALICE! WITHOUT THIS MEASURELESS AND PERPETUAL UNCERTAINTY, THE DRAMA OF HUMAN LIFE WOULD BE DESTROYED.

1948

LET US BE CONTENTED WITH WHAT HAS HAPPENED TO US AND THANKFUL FOR ALL WE HAVE BEEN SPARED.

1931

EVIDENTLY HE HAD THE FIRST QUALITY OF AN ANGLER, WHICH IS NOT TO MEASURE THE PLEASURE BY THE CATCH.

1951

EVERYONE CAN HELP IN SOME WAY OR OTHER.

1947

NOURISH YOUR HOPES, BUT DO NOT OVERLOOK REALITIES.

1935

YOU DON'T WANT TO KNOCK A MAN DOWN EXCEPT TO PICK HIM UP IN A BETTER FRAME OF MIND.

1949

ONE OUGHT TO BE JUST BEFORE ONE IS GENEROUS.

1947

PLANT A GARDEN IN WHICH YOU CAN SIT WHEN DIGGING DAYS ARE DONE.

1921

THE ART OF POLITICS

WHAT IS THE USE OF LIVING, IF IT BE NOT TO STRIVE FOR NOBLE CAUSES AND TO MAKE THIS MUDDLED WORLD A BETTER PLACE FOR THOSE WHO WILL LIVE IN IT AFTER WE ARE GONE?

1908

IT IS ALWAYS MORE EASY TO DISCOVER AND PROCLAIM GENERAL PRINCIPLES THAN TO APPLY THEM.

1936

WE SHALL NOT BE JUDGED BY THE CRITICISMS OF OUR OPPONENTS, BUT BY THE CONSEQUENCES OF OUR ACTS.

1926

RARE AND PRECIOUS IS THE TRULY DISINTERESTED MAN.

1899

IT IS EASIER TO BREAK CROCKERY THAN TO MEND IT.

1948

PERFECT SOLUTIONS TO OUR DIFFICULTIES ARE NOT TO BE LOOKED FOR IN AN IMPERFECT WORLD.

1951

IN POLITICS, WHEN YOU ARE IN DOUBT WHAT TO DO, DO NOTHING ... WHEN YOU ARE IN DOUBT WHAT TO SAY, SAY WHAT YOU REALLY THINK.

1905

POLITICIANS RISE BY TOILS AND STRUGGLES. THEY EXPECT TO FALL; THEY HOPE TO RISE AGAIN.

1931

IT IS A FINE THING TO BE HONEST, BUT IT IS VERY IMPORTANT FOR A PRIME MINISTER TO BE RIGHT.

1923

THE FINEST COMBINATION IN THE WORLD IS POWER AND MERCY. THE WORST COMBINATION IN THE WORLD IS WEAKNESS AND STRIFE.

1919

THE INHERENT VICE OF CAPITALISM IS THE UNEQUAL SHARING OF BLESSINGS. THE INHERENT VIRTUE OF SOCIALISM IS THE EQUAL SHARING OF MISERIES.

1945

TOO OFTEN THE STRONG, SILENT MAN IS SILENT ONLY BECAUSE HE DOES NOT KNOW WHAT TO SAY, AND HE IS REPUTED STRONG ONLY BECAUSE HE HAS REMAINED SILENT.

1924

ONE CAN ALWAYS CONSULT A MAN AND ASK HIM 'WOULD YOU LIKE YOUR HEAD CUT OFF TOMORROW?' AND AFTER HE HAS SAID 'I WOULD RATHER NOT,' CUT IT OFF. 'CONSULTATION' IS A VAGUE AND ELASTIC TERM.

1947

[A POLITICIAN NEEDS...] THE ABILITY TO FORETELL WHAT IS GOING TO HAPPEN TOMORROW, NEXT WEEK, NEXT MONTH AND NEXT YEAR – AND TO HAVE THE ABILITY AFTERWARDS TO EXPLAIN WHY IT DIDN'T HAPPEN.

1902

AFTER THINGS ARE OVER IT IS EASY TO CHOOSE THE FINE MENTAL AND MORAL POSITIONS WHICH ONE SHOULD ADOPT.

1950

PERSEVERE TOWARDS THOSE OBJECTIVES WHICH ARE LIGHTED FOR US BY ALL THE WISDOM AND INSPIRATION OF THE PAST.

1948

PERHAPS IT IS BETTER TO BE IRRESPONSIBLE AND RIGHT THAN TO BE RESPONSIBLE AND WRONG.

1950

THERE IS NO WORSE MISTAKE IN PUBLIC LEADERSHIP THAN TO HOLD OUT FALSE HOPES SOON TO BE SWEPT AWAY. THE BRITISH PEOPLE CAN FACE PERIL OR MISFORTUNE WITH FORTITUDE AND BUOYANCY, BUT THEY BITTERLY RESENT

BEING DECEIVED OR FINDING THAT THOSE RESPONSIBLE FOR THEIR AFFAIRS ARE THEMSELVES DWELLING IN A FOOL'S PARADISE.

1951

IT IS BETTER TO BE BOTH RIGHT AND CONSISTENT. BUT IF YOU HAVE TO CHOOSE – YOU MUST CHOOSE TO BE RIGHT.

1952

IT WOULD BE A GREAT REFORM IN POLITICS IF WISDOM COULD BE MADE TO SPREAD AS EASILY AND AS RAPIDLY AS FOLLY.

1947

THE ART OF WAR

NOTHING IN LIFE IS SO EXHILARATING AS TO BE SHOT AT WITHOUT RESULT.

1898

THERE IS ONLY ONE THING WORSE THAN FIGHTING WITH ALLIES, AND THAT IS FIGHTING WITHOUT THEM.

1945

WE MAY HAVE TAKEN DECISIONS WHICH WILL PROVE TO BE LESS GOOD THAN WE HOPED, BUT AT ANY RATE ANYTHING IS BETTER THAN NOT HAVING A PLAN.

1943

A BEAR IN THE FOREST IS A PROPER MATTER FOR SPECULATION; A BEAR IN THE ZOO IS A PROPER MATTER FOR PUBLIC CURIOSITY; A BEAR IN YOUR WIFE'S BED IS A MATTER OF THE GRAVEST CONCERN.

1951 in respect of Stalin's appetite for expansion.

EXCEPT IN SO FAR AS FORCE IS CONCERNED, THERE IS NO EQUALITY BETWEEN RIGHT AND WRONG.

1945

IN WARTIME, TRUTH IS SO PRECIOUS THAT SHE SHOULD ALWAYS BE ATTENDED BY A BODYGUARD OF LIES.

1943

WHEN WE FACE WITH A STEADY EYE THE DIFFICULTIES WHICH LIE BEFORE US, WE MAY DERIVE NEW CONFIDENCE FROM REMEMBERING THOSE WE HAVE ALREADY OVERCOME.

1941

IT IS MUCH BETTER TO BE FRIGHTENED NOW THAN TO BE KILLED HEREAFTER.

1934

TO TRY TO BE SAFE EVERYWHERE IS TO BE STRONG NOWHERE.

1951

CONSIDERATION FOR THE LIVES OF OTHERS AND THE LAWS OF HUMANITY, EVEN WHEN ONE IS STRUGGLING FOR ONE'S LIFE AND IN THE GREATEST STRESS, DOES NOT GO WHOLLY UNREWARDED.

1917

STRENGTH IN ADVERSITY

HOW OFTEN IN LIFE MUST ONE BE CONTENT WITH WHAT ONE CAN GET!

1943

WE MUST BE READY, AS WE ALWAYS HAVE BEEN READY, TO TAKE THE ROUGH WITH THE SMOOTH.

1941

IN CRITICAL AND BAFFLING SITUATIONS IT IS ALWAYS BEST TO RECUR TO FIRST PRINCIPLES AND SIMPLE ACTION.

1951

WE HAVE A LOT OF ANXIETIES, AND ONE CANCELS OUT ANOTHER VERY OFTEN.

1943

STRENGTH IS GRANTED TO US ALL WHEN WE ARE NEEDED TO SERVE GREAT CAUSES.

1946

THERE IS ALWAYS A STRONG CASE FOR DOING NOTHING, ESPECIALLY FOR DOING NOTHING YOURSELF.

1923

IT IS A CRIME TO DESPAIR. WE MUST LEARN TO DRAW FROM MISFORTUNE THE MEANS OF FUTURE STRENGTH.

1938

SO WE HAVE HAD TO DISPENSE WITH THE INDISPENSABLE.

1922

ONE ALWAYS MEASURES FRIENDSHIPS BY HOW THEY SHOW UP IN BAD WEATHER.

1948

I DO NOT ADMIRE PEOPLE WHO ARE WISE AFTER THE EVENT. I WOULD RATHER BE IMPALED ON THE OTHER HORN OF THE DILEMMA AND BE CALLED ONE OF THE 'I TOLD YOU SO'S.'

1935

WE REMEMBER THE SARDONIC WAR-TIME JOKE ABOUT THE OPTIMIST AND THE PESSIMIST. THE OPTIMIST WAS THE MAN WHO DID NOT MIND WHAT HAPPENED SO LONG AS IT DID NOT HAPPEN TO HIM. THE PESSIMIST WAS THE MAN WHO LIVED WITH THE OPTIMIST.

1938

IT IS A GREAT MISTAKE TO SUPPOSE THAT THRIFT IS CAUSED ONLY BY FEAR; IT SPRINGS FROM HOPE AS WELL AS FROM FEAR; WHERE THERE IS NO HOPE, BE SURE THERE WILL BE NO THRIFT.

1908

ENOUGH IS AS GOOD AS A FEAST.

1918

I HAVE A REMEDY FOR WORRIES THAT ALWAYS WORKS. NEVER LET ONE WORRY, NO MATTER HOW GREAT, BE IN YOUR MIND ALL ALONE. IT WILL DRIVE YOU MAD. GIVE IT COMPANY, PREFERABLY SOMETHING SMALLER, AND WRITE IT DOWN ON A PIECE OF

PAPER. THEN YOU WILL SPEND SOME TIME THINKING ABOUT THE SECOND WORRY, AND THE FIRST ONE WILL GRADUALLY DIMINISH.

1951

WE MUST JUST KBO.

1941

Churchill's familiar maxim, usually delivered to colleagues and family, and abbreviated in polite company. It stood for 'Keep Buggering On'.

REFLECTIONS

USUALLY YOUTH IS FOR FREEDOM AND REFORM, MATURITY FOR JUDICIOUS COMPROMISE, AND OLD AGE FOR STABILITY AND REPOSE.

1927

THE WORST QUARRELS ONLY ARISE WHEN BOTH SIDES ARE EQUALLY IN THE RIGHT AND IN THE WRONG.

1936

A WOMAN IS AS OLD AS SHE LOOKS; A MAN IS AS OLD AS HE FEELS; AND A BOY IS AS OLD AS HE IS TREATED.

1942

BROADLY SPEAKING, HUMAN BEINGS MAY BE DIVIDED INTO THREE CLASSES: THOSE WHO ARE BILLED TO DEATH, THOSE WHO ARE WORRIED TO DEATH, AND THOSE WHO ARE BORED TO DEATH.

1925

A NATION WITHOUT A CONSCIENCE IS A NATION WITHOUT A SOUL. A NATION WITHOUT A SOUL IS A NATION THAT CANNOT LIVE.

1951

THE WORLD WOULD BE BETTER OFF IF IT WERE INHABITED ONLY BY ANIMALS.

1946

THOUGHT ARISING FROM FACTUAL EXPERIENCE MAY BE A BRIDLE OR A SPUR.

1952

THE GLORY OF LIGHT CANNOT EXIST WITHOUT ITS SHADOWS.

1931

YOU SHOULD NEVER HARNESS A THOROUGHBRED TO A DUNG CART.

1942

JUSTICE MOVES SLOWLY AND REMORSELESSLY UPON ITS PATH, BUT IT REACHES ITS GOAL EVENTUALLY.

1929

SELF-REFLECTION

WE ARE ALL WORMS. BUT I DO BELIEVE THAT I AM A GLOW-WORM.

1906

WHEN I WAS YOUNGER I MADE IT A RULE NEVER TO TAKE STRONG DRINK BEFORE LUNCH. IT IS NOW MY RULE NEVER TO DO SO BEFORE BREAKFAST.

1952

I COULD NOT LIVE WITHOUT CHAMPAGNE. IN VICTORY I DESERVE IT. IN DEFEAT I NEED IT.

1946

I HAVE DERIVED CONTINUED BENEFIT FROM CRITICISM AT ALL PERIODS OF MY LIFE AND I DO NOT REMEMBER ANY TIME WHEN I WAS EVER SHORT OF IT.

1914

I AM ALWAYS READY TO LEARN, ALTHOUGH I DO NOT ALWAYS LIKE BEING TAUGHT.

1952

IN THE COURSE OF MY LIFE I HAVE OFTEN HAD TO EAT MY WORDS, AND I MUST CONFESS THAT I HAVE ALWAYS FOUND IT A WHOLESOME DIET.

1940

I ALWAYS PREFER TO ACCEPT THE GUIDANCE OF MY HEART TO CALCULATIONS OF PUBLIC FEELING.

1937

I GET MY EXERCISE SERVING AS PALL-BEARER TO MY MANY FRIENDS WHO EXERCISED ALL THEIR LIVES.

1950

THE JOURNEY HAS BEEN ENJOYABLE AND WELL WORTH THE TAKING – ONCE.

1931

READ MORE
WISE WORDS FROM
SIR WINSTON
CHURCHILL ...

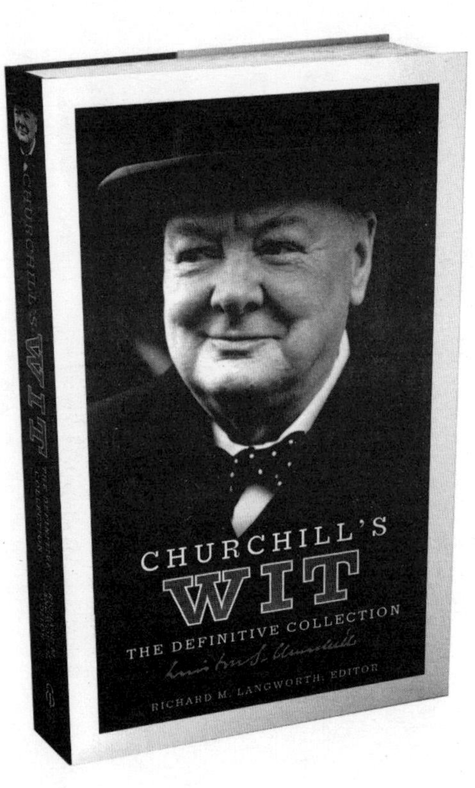
CHURCHILL'S
WIT
THE DEFINITIVE COLLECTION
RICHARD M. LANGWORTH, EDITOR

THE PATRIOT'S CHURCHILL
AN INSPIRING COLLECTION OF CHURCHILL'S FINEST WORDS
RICHARD M. LANGWORTH, EDITOR

THE PATRIOT'S CHURCHILL
RICHARD M. LANGWORTH, EDITOR
AN INSPIRING COLLECTION OF CHURCHILL'S FINEST WORDS

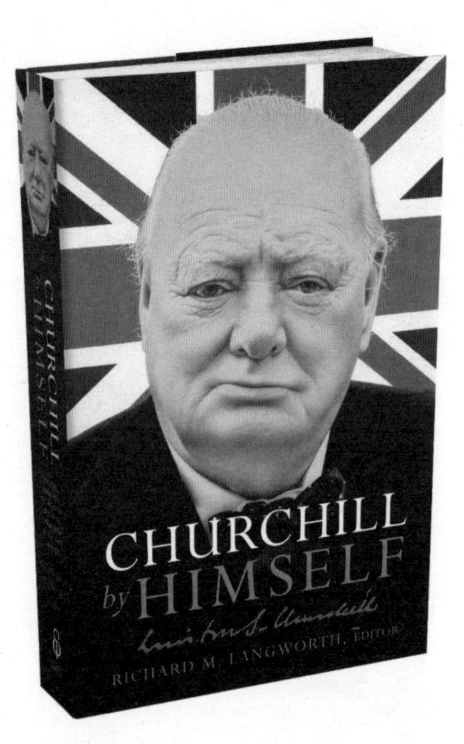
CHURCHILL
by HIMSELF
RICHARD M. LANGWORTH, EDITOR
CHURCHILL by HIMSELF